SUPERMAN
AND THE UTOPIA ON URANUS

A SOLAR SYSTEM ADVENTURE

by Steve Korté
illustrated by Dario Brizuela
Superman created by Jerry Siegel and Joe Shuster
by special arrangement with the Jerry Siegel family

Consultant:
Steve Kortenkamp, PhD
Associate Professor of Practice
Lunar and Planetary Lab
University of Arizona
Tucson, Arizona

CAPSTONE PRESS
a capstone imprint

WHOOOSH!

Superman zooms through the sky above the city of Metropolis.

The Man of Steel isn't looking for criminals. He has received a call from Professor Emil Hamilton at S.T.A.R. Labs. The professor asked Superman to come to the world-famous scientific laboratory as quickly as possible.

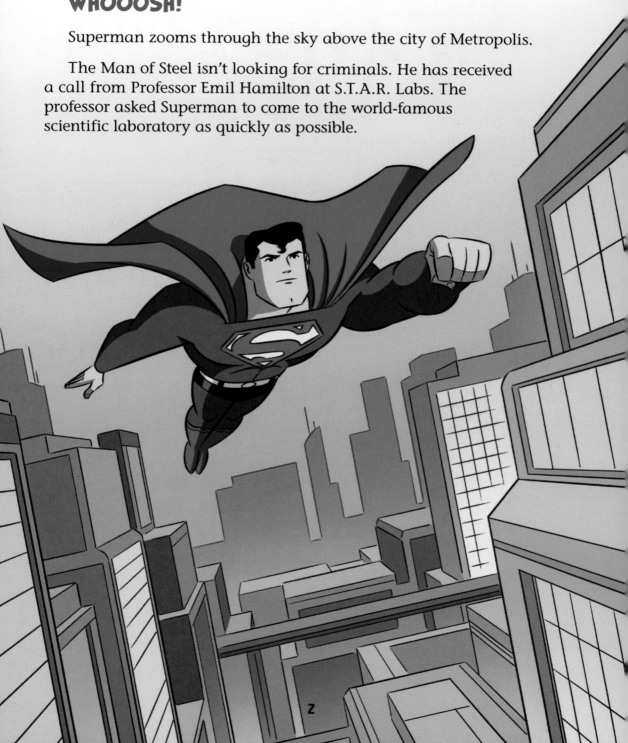

Inside S.T.A.R. Labs, Superman and Professor Hamilton walk to a door labeled "Top Secret."

"This is our Aeronautics and Space Division," says Hamilton as he types a security code into a control panel. The door opens, and he leads Superman into the room.

"I have a mission for you," says Hamilton, pointing at a pale blue world on a large video screen. Superman recognizes it as Uranus, the seventh planet from the Sun.

Fact
Most scientists pronounce Uranus as "YOOR-uh-nuhs." For many years the planet's name was pronounced as "yoo-REY-nuhs."

"Eleven years ago we launched the *Wayfarer* spacecraft," says Hamilton. "It sent us spectacular images of Jupiter and Saturn, the two largest planets in our solar system."

Superman points to the video screen and asks, "And what about Uranus, the next planet after them?"

"That's just it," Hamilton replies, changing the image on the screen. "The *Wayfarer* is now traveling past Uranus. It has detected something unusual."

"Unusual?" asks Superman with surprise.

"The spacecraft sent back images of something very small traveling through the planet's frigid atmosphere," says Hamilton. "We can't tell what it is."

"Could it be an asteroid?" asks Superman.

"No," says Hamilton. "The unknown object is traveling both to *and* from Uranus. The spacecraft even spotted an object flying toward Miranda, one of the planet's many moons."

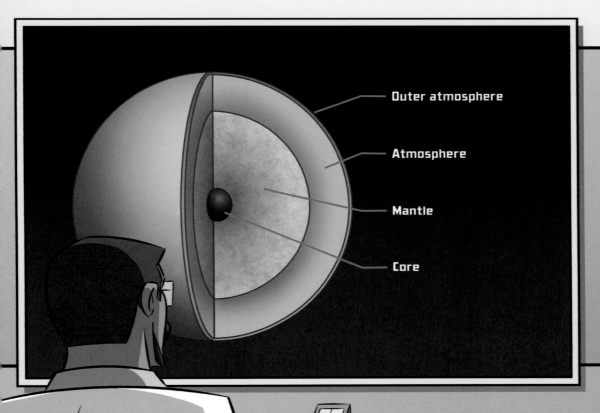

Outer atmosphere

Atmosphere

Mantle

Core

Superman frowns. "Professor, Uranus has no solid surface, right?"

"Correct," says Hamilton. "The sky above Uranus is made up of hydrogen and helium gas. The planet itself is made up of a liquid mixture of water, ammonia, and methane surrounding a solid rocky core."

The image changes again. Superman studies a dark band of rings circling the planet.

"Maybe the mystery object came from these rings that are in such an unusual position?" he asks.

"No, those 13 rings are made up of tightly packed chunks of ice and rocks," says Hamilton. "And they are standing upright for good reason. Unlike every other planet in our solar system, Uranus travels around the Sun tilted on its side. Long ago, the planet may have been knocked over by a powerful blow from a large object."

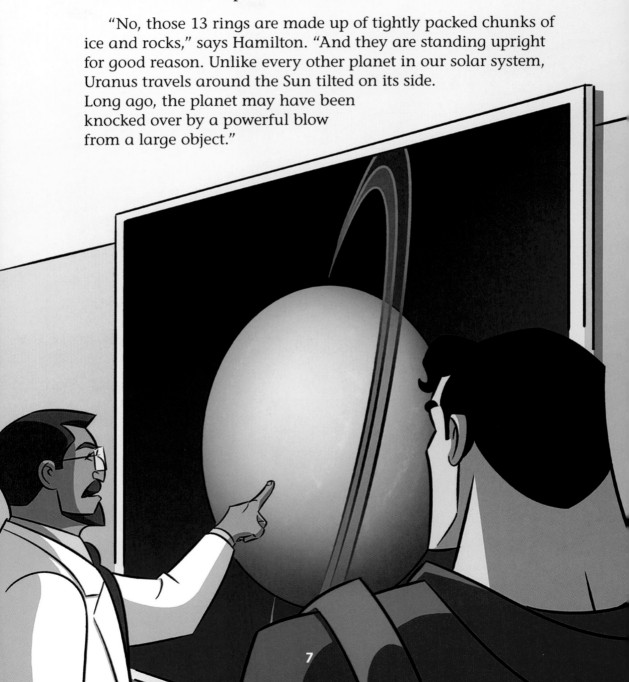

The image on the screen changes to a dark world. Its surface is covered in jagged cracks next to deep canyons and tall ridges.

"This is Miranda, one of Uranus' moons," says Hamilton. "It's only about 300 miles, or 500 kilometers, across. But it is one of the most unusual worlds in our solar system. The surface is covered with dark, jagged areas next to light icy patches."

Fact
Uranus has 27 moons.
Miranda is the smallest of the
planet's five major moons.
The remaining 22 moons are
even smaller than Miranda.

Hamilton changes the image on the screen and points to a towering ridge on Miranda.

"One of the tallest cliffs in our solar system is on Miranda," he says. "Verona Rupes is almost 6 miles, or 10 kilometers, high. That's taller than Mount Everest on Earth!"

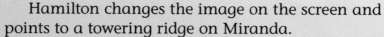

"And why are you showing me this?" asks the Man of Steel.

"Because our spacecraft has detected the formation of a new crater on Miranda," Hamilton says, his voice growing serious. "Whatever is flying around Uranus may have also created a new hole in this moon."

Professor Hamilton turns to Superman. "We need you to find out what is going on," he says.

Superman says goodbye to Professor Hamilton and steps outside S.T.A.R. Labs. Seconds later, the Man of Steel launches himself into the air.

With a burst of super-speed, Superman rockets past the Moon, Mars, Jupiter, and Saturn. Soon he draws closer to the freezing cold world of Uranus.

Superman floats in space as he approaches the 13 dark, rocky rings that orbit Uranus. He studies the giant, pale blue world.

What sort of creature could be traveling within the slushy mixture of water and gases that covers Uranus? wonders the Man of Steel.

Fact
Sunlight reflecting off methane gas in Uranus' atmosphere gives the planet its unusual pale blue color.

Superman turns back to look at the Sun. It is almost 2 billion miles (3.2 billion km) away and looks like a very bright star. He remembers that Professor Hamilton told him that Uranus is a very cold planet. The clouds covering the planet have an average temperature of minus 357 degrees Fahrenheit (minus 216 degrees Celsius).

Superman then flies close to Miranda. He hovers over the dark surface of the moon. Miranda is covered with jagged black areas next to patches of ice. There are also oval patterns that look like racetracks. The Man of Steel swoops down to Verona Rupes, the moon's giant cliff.

To his surprise, Superman sees a giant cave has been carved into the icy wall at the bottom of the ridge. He flies closer to investigate.

Fact

Miranda's jagged look is a mystery. It may have been smashed apart by a large object and then come back together. Or long ago, the rocky pieces of the moon were pulled toward its center while the icy pieces pushed outward.

Superman cautiously enters the cave. When his eyes adjust to the dim light, he is amazed. Dark, ice-cold rocks are arranged in patterns on the floor of the cave.

The rocks have been piled up to form chairs and tables. At one end of the cave, the rocks have been stacked together to create a large bed.

Superman shakes his head with puzzlement. Someone or some *thing* has been living inside this cave on Miranda!

Superman flies away from Miranda and heads toward Uranus.

He passes through the frozen methane atmosphere that surrounds Uranus and sinks down into the planet's interior.

The Man of Steel searches through the soupy mixture of water, ammonia, and methane that makes up Uranus.

He wonders what he is going to find.

Suddenly, Superman discovers Bizarro floating on his back. The strange-looking villain snores as he takes a nap.

Bizarro is an imperfect clone of Superman. He does everything backward. When he tries to be a hero like Superman, he always gets everything wrong.

Years ago, Superman talked Bizarro into moving to Bizarro World. This distant, square-shaped planet was home to other strange Bizarro-like creatures. Bizarro also promised Superman that he would return to Earth only once a year.

"Uranus is no place for you to live," Superman says with a frown.

"Me love to breathe ammonia and methane here," Bizarro says happily. "Much tastier than boring oxygen on Earth. And me also like living on planet tilted over on its side."

"And what about your cave on Miranda?" asks Superman with a sigh.

"Oh, Superman saw my new home?" the creature says with a smile. "Me love Miranda moon. It cracked and jagged just like Bizarro's face."

"I'm sorry, but you have to go back to Bizarro World," says Superman firmly.

"Me no have to go anywhere," Bizarro says stubbornly. "Me good hero, and me as strong as Superman!"

"Bizarro, you are not—" begins Superman.

"Not as strong as Superman?" interrupts Bizarro. "Me prove it!"

Suddenly, the villain shoves the Man of Steel. Together they zoom through Uranus' outer atmosphere and toward a moon named Cordelia.

Fact
Cordelia is the closest moon to Uranus. It is one of the planet's smallest moons, at only 25 miles (40 km) wide.

BLAM!

Superman crashes onto Cordelia. With a laugh, Bizarro flies away.

Superman quickly jumps to his feet and launches himself away from Cordelia's icy surface.

Soon he flies through the Epsilon ring, one of the 13 rings that surround Uranus.

Superman strains to see through the rocks and ice floating within the ring. A few larger boulders even bounce harmlessly off the Man of Steel's body.

Exiting the Epsilon ring,
Superman sees Bizarro standing on
Ophelia, the next closest moon.

CRUNCH!

Bizarro rips up a giant chunk of ice and throws it at Superman.

ZAP!

The Man of Steel melts the ice with his heat-vision.

"We see who is faster, Bizarro or Superman," the villain yells. Then
he launches into space and heads toward Cressida, the next moon.

Superman sighs. He doesn't want to chase Bizarro to all 27 moons
of Uranus.

24

As they fly toward Cressida, Superman notices Bizarro glancing toward the Sun. The Man of Steel has an idea.

"Bizarro, wait just a minute," calls out Superman. "Do you remember promising to return to Earth only once a year?"

"Yes, that am true," agrees the villain. "Bizarro can tell that a year has passed when Earth travels one time all the way around the Sun."

"That's exactly right, Bizarro," Superman says.

"I have a job for you," says Superman. "How about if you guard Uranus for one year? You can visit me in Metropolis after Uranus travels once all the way around the Sun."

A confused look comes over Bizarro's face. He is worried that it might be a trick.

"If Bizarro agree, me can still call Uranus home?" the villain asks.

"Sure," replies Superman. "It's all yours."

"That seem like a good deal," says Bizarro. "Me going to guard Uranus as it goes around the Sun. When it make one whole trip, me come to Metropolis to check on Superman!"

"Goodbye, Superman," calls out Bizarro as he zooms away. "Me have guard duty on Uranus."

What Bizarro doesn't know is that it takes 84 Earth years for Uranus to orbit once around the Sun.

Superman waves goodbye and heads back to Metropolis. With luck, his plan may just keep Bizarro busy for 84 years!

MORE ABOUT URANUS

- William Herschel and his sister Caroline were amateur astronomers. In 1781, they looked through their homemade telescope and discovered the seventh planet from the Sun.

- Some people wanted to name Herschel's new discovery "Planet Herschel." But Herschel wanted to name the planet "Georgium Sidus," after England's King George.

- In 1850, the planet was officially named for Uranus, the Greek god of the sky. All of the other planets are named after mythological gods too.

- Uranus is the third-largest planet in the solar system. It is also about four times wider than Earth. In fact, if Earth were as wide as a dime, Uranus would be as wide as the top of a coffee mug.

- Titania is Uranus' largest moon. It is about half the size of Earth's moon.

- Uranus' moon Miranda has a very low gravity. If an astronaut could drop a rock from its highest cliff, the rock would take 10 minutes to reach the ground.

- All 27 of Uranus' moons are named for characters in plays by the famous playwright William Shakespeare.

- Only the five largest moons of Uranus are completely round worlds. The 22 smaller ones are more irregularly shaped.

- The Epsilon ring is one of the 13 known rings orbiting Uranus. It is surrounded by the orbits of two moons, Cordelia and Ophelia. Their gravity keeps the Epsilon ring in place.

- NASA's *Voyager 2* has been the only spacecraft to fly close to Uranus. It was launched in 1977, and nine years later it came within 50,640 miles (81,500 km) of the planet. *Voyager 2* was the only spacecraft to study all four of our solar system's giant gas planets.

aeronautics (ayr-uh-NAW-tiks)—the science and practice of designing and building aircraft

ammonia (uh-moh-NEE-uh)—a gas that is made up of nitrogen and hydrogen

asteroid (AS-tuh-royd)—a large space rock that moves around the Sun

atmosphere (AT-muhss-fihr)—the layer of gases that surrounds some planets, dwarf planets, and moons

crater (KRAY-tuhr)—a hole made when large pieces of rock crash into a planet or moon's surface

helium (HEE-lee-uhm)—a lightweight, colorless gas that does not burn

hydrogen (HYE-druh-juhn)—a colorless gas that is lighter than air and burns easily

methane (meth-AYN)—a colorless, flammable gas; methane becomes a liquid at extremely cold temperatures

orbit (OR-bit)—the path an object follows while circling another object in space

solar system (SOH-lur SISS-tuhm)—the Sun and the objects that move around it

Adamson, Thomas. *The Secrets of Uranus.* Smithsonian Planets. North Mankato, Minn.: Capstone Press, 2016.

Black, Vanessa. *Uranus.* Space Voyager. Minneapolis: Bullfrog Books, 2018.

Keiser, Cody. *Exploring Uranus.* Journey Through Our Solar System. New York: KidHaven Publishing, 2018.

TITLES IN THIS SET

INDEX

INTERNET SITES

Use FactHound to find Internet sites related to this book.
Visit *www.facthound.com*
Just type in 9781543515732 and go.

Published by Capstone Press in 2018
1710 Roe Crest Drive
North Mankato, Minnesota 56003
www.mycapstone.com

Cataloging-in-publication information is on file with the Library of Congress.
ISBN 978-1-5435-1573-2 (library binding)
ISBN 978-1-5435-1581-7 (paperback)
ISBN 978-1-5435-1589-3 (eBook PDF)

Editorial Credits
Christopher Harbo, editor; Kayla Rossow, designer; Laura Manthe, production specialist

Summary: Superman squares off against the super-villain Bizarro in an adventure that reveals the
remarkable features and characteristics of the planet Uranus and its moons.

Illustration Credits
Gregg Schigiel (Superman): back cover, 1, 32

Printed in the United States of America.
PA017